This book belongs to:

____

____

____

Nathaniel was a very popular boy at school. He always looked smart, brushed his teeth, oiled and brushed his hair until it was smooth and shiny. He ate lots of healthy food and got plenty of sleep. He was so handsome!

Nathaniel was a very popular boy at school.
He always looked smart, brushed his teeth,
oiled and brushed his hair until it was smooth
and shiny. He ate lots of healthy food and got
plenty of sleep. He was so handsome!

Nathaniel was well behaved at school and did his reading every night at home. He was good at building models with Lego such as cars, trucks and buildings.

LEGO

Nathaniel made friends at church and would go camping with them. He learned skills such as putting up tents, tying knots and the names of stars in the galaxy.

He received his honours badges and was proud of his achievements.

His parents clapped enthusiastically when he received his awards. His Mummy attached the patches and badges to his forest-green coloured sash.

Nathaniel soon made friends at school. He would go to basketball practice and his Daddy would meet other parents who told him that they thought he was good at the sport as he tackled other players and dribbled the ball to score a basket.

His father praised him for playing well with the other children and being considerate towards them without being rough.

Nathaniel soon made friends at school. He would go to basketball practice and his Daddy would meet other parents who told him that they thought he was good at the sport as he tackled other players and dribbled the ball to score a basket.

His father praised him for playing well with the other children and being considerate towards them without being rough.

Nathaniel soon made friends at school. He would go to basketball practice and his Daddy would meet other parents who told him that they thought he was good at the sport as he tackled other players and dribbled the ball to score a basket.

His father praised him for playing well with the other children and being considerate towards them without being rough.

When he was at home, Nathaniel had the opportunity to practice the brand new techniques he had learnt, on some of his friends. Some wanted "fades" and others wanted "line-ups".

Their parents gave permission for the new styles and Nathaniel made sure that they were suitable for school.

Nathaniel realised that people enjoyed looking smart, especially when they attended events such as baby christenings, weddings and graduations.

He saw that he could have a positive impact on people's lives by using the skills he had been learning.

19

After finishing secondary school, Nathaniel attended a local college for two years where he learned how to use the right tools for cutting hair, how to create plaits and take care of locks.

He was so proud to receive his diploma that he could not stop smiling all day!

Once he was qualified, Nathaniel managed to get a job as a barber with a cruise ship company.

He flew a very long distance from his home to Australia and from there he spent nine months working on a big cruise ship that travelled from Australia to Thailand, Singapore and Malaysia.

He visited famous sights and monuments, met friendly people and tasted the delicious food they cooked. He enjoyed swimming in the beautifully warm, turquoise seas.

Nathaniel worked alongside other barbers
and hairdressers to help the guests on their
holidays look their very best.

He met people from around the world and
learned about their languages, cultures and
heritage.

He even learned some Spanish and
 French words and used them to
make new friends.

Salon

Eventually Nathaniel came back home to work and help the people in his home city, Birmingham.

He would cut the hair of children who were shy and a little bit frightened about sitting on the booster cushion in the big red chair with the shiny arms.

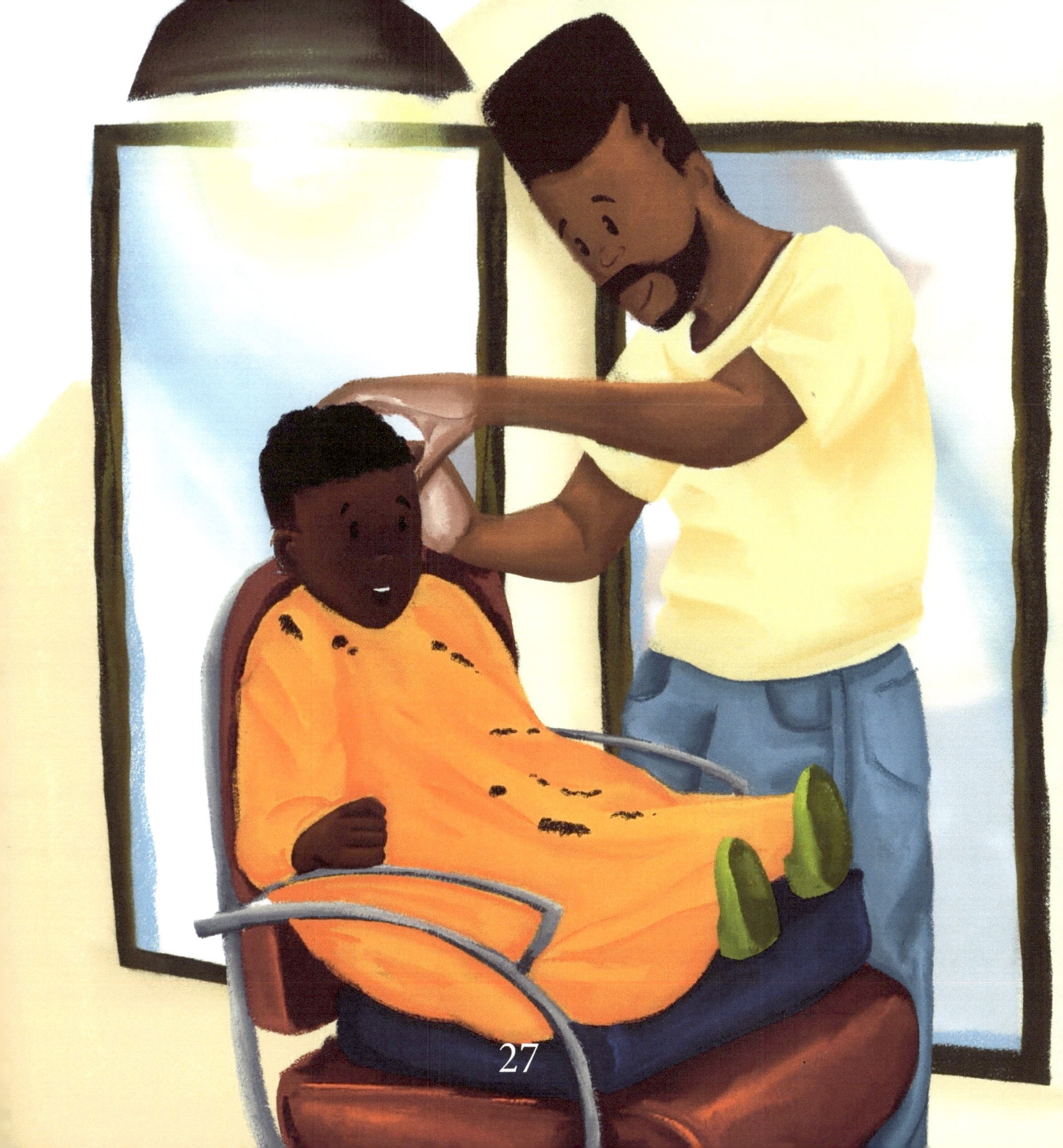

Nathaniel still works hard as a barber. He has his own salon in the high street near his home. He helps to train other people to become barbers. He has become an independent businessman!

NATHANIEL'S BARBER SHOP
Now Open !
29

Nathaniel always takes the time to listen to his customers who want to share information about the things in their lives that make them happy and sad.

He goes to the homeless people and into care homes where older people and those with disabilities live, so that they feel cared for too!

So, as you can see Nathaniel is a brilliant barber! He cares for his customers in lots of ways!

Maybe you can make the people around you feel looked after too, and if you want be a kind barber just like Nathaniel, then you can do it too!

If you want to be the best barber take a look at these references to learn how!

<u>For Kids:</u>

Kiddle
A webiste packed full of information about the barbering profession for young kids.
https://kids.kiddle.co/Barber

kidadl
15 Interesting Barber Facts That You Probably Didn't Know About!
https://kidadl.com/facts/interesting-barber-facts-that-you-probably-didn-t-know-about

PBS Kids
Hair styling game, great fun for young kids.
https://pbskids.org/peg/games/hair-salon/

<u>For parents and guardians:</u>

National careers service information page on barbering careers
 https://nationalcareers.service.gov.uk/job-profiles/barber

Barbercourses.com: covers the top-rated non-university barbering
courses in the UK.
 https://barbercourses.com/uk/

The Complete University Guide page on university hairdressing courses.
https://www.thecompleteuniversityguide.co.uk/courses/search/
undergraduate/hairdressing

What do you want to be when you grow up? Draw it below!

Notes!

Check out some other books in the series!

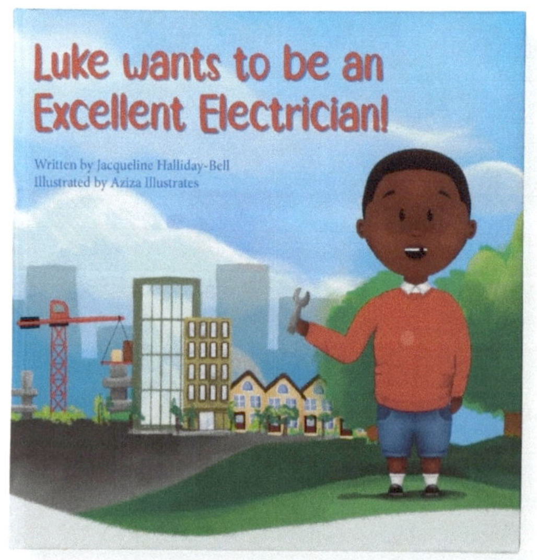